TRAVELING TOGETHER

Other Books by David Haney:

Couples in Mission and Ministry
    (with Aileen Haney)
The Lord and His Laity
Bold New Laity (editor)
Journey Into Life
Renewal Reminders (with James Mahoney)
Breakthrough Into Renewal
The Idea of the Laity
Renew My Church

TRAVELING TOGETHER

Love Letters for Couples

David and Aileen Haney

ZONDERVAN
PUBLISHING HOUSE
OF THE ZONDERVAN CORPORATION
GRAND RAPIDS, MICHIGAN 49506

TRAVELING TOGETHER: Love Letters for Couples
Copyright © 1983 by The Zondervan Corporation
Grand Rapids, Michigan

Edited by Linda DeVries
Designed by Carole B. Parrish

Scripture quotations are from *The Holy Bible: The New International Version*, copyright © 1978 by the New York International Bible Society, unless otherwise indicated.

Library of Congress Cataloging in Publication Data

Haney, David.
    Traveling together.

    1. Married people—Prayer-books and devotions—English. I. Haney, Aileen. II. Title.

| BV4845.H36 | 1983 | 242'.64 | 83-14588 |

ISBN 0-310-46931-7

Printed in the United States of America

83 84 85 86 87 88 89 / 9 8 7 6 5 4 3 2 1

For

Willard and Wilma

Contents

Introduction

I deliberately waited until this particular time and place to write this introduction for it has unusual significance. I wanted to conclude the book here on the beautiful French West Indies island of Guadeloupe.

Aileen and I are celebrating our *twenty-fifth wedding anniversary*—twenty-five years en route together.

That a book should mark our silver anniversary is both natural and planned. It is natural in that writing has been so much a part of our lives. Since 1972, every vacation we have taken has been a "writing vacation." All year long I would gather the ideas and information for a book; and then, on vacation, I would write it. Up at daylight, I would write until noon and then rejoin my family for the rest of the day.

Thus, from the beach at Ocean City, Maryland (*Renew My Church* and *Breakthrough Into Renewal*), to the Blue Ridge Mountains of North Carolina (*The Idea of the Laity*) to the Sangre de Cristo Mountains of New Mexico (*Renewal Reminders* and *Bold New Laity*), to Malibu (*Couples in Mission and Ministry*), to the Swiss Alps (*Journey Into Life*), the books have come. As you can see, we enjoy mountains and beaches. Only one (*The Lord and His Laity*) was written at home.

Traveling Together was planned too, at least after a fashion. For a number of years my ministry has kept me on the road about half the time, all across the nation and in various parts of the world. When I started traveling I began the habit of writing letters to Aileen while I was *en route*. Upon my return I would give them to her to read. We both enjoyed the habit.

After several years we shared this "secret" of ours in a couples' retreat we were leading. Their interest was immediate. After that we shared a few of the letters here and there and repeatedly heard that we should put them into print. We had been struggling with what to write to mark our silver anniversary and we wanted it to be something done together. Thus this book seemed natural. The conviction that this was "it" continued to grow. And here it is!

Aileen's role was to cull the stack for thirty-one letters, enough for one full month of devotions. They were to be comprehensive, covering the whole of life and its concerns. I would then edit them while she added the activities (discussion and Scripture suggestions) to each. Together, then, we share our joint effort.

Our prayer is that these bits and pieces from our journey together will be of help to you in yours. If you, the readers, enjoy them, it is a plus to our reward. For, you see, our reward came as we did them together.

David P. Haney
Guadeloupe, F.W.I., 1982

How to Use This Book

One of the challenges my husband, David, and I have faced over the years is that of finding new and interesting ways to have a daily devotional time together. With this book we feel we have responded favorably to that challenge.

There is specific purpose for this book. It is designed to be used as a *daily devotional guide for couples*. There are thirty-one selections—enough for one full month of devotions together. Our suggestion is that you set aside some time together early in the morning or before retiring at night. One of you read the selection, the other the Scripture passage. Then discuss the questions at the end of the selection. Finally—and most importantly—pray together.

The book may also be used for *personal devotions*, of course. It can easily be adapted and used by *couples' groups* as well.

Most of all, we pray that the Lord will use this book—and you—in an enriching and meaningful way.

David and I have led couples' retreats for many years now and have found a real hunger among couples who attend for that elusive "something more" in their marriages. We have had various kinds of couples' emphases and classes in the churches we have served and always found the audiences and groups easy to form. The need is there.

We have also watched the volumes of couples' books compounded, especially over the past few years. Many of them are good, some excellent, but most are theoretical. Likewise, many of them are extremely authoritative, some even being written by those with no authoritative personal experience, with the authors themselves being single. While this is not essentially nullifying, it does make one's "authority" at least less than authoritative. Yet, for all that, there are enough books of "expert advice."

One thing we have noticed is the absence of the oldest form of Christian witness: the first-person account. But how could we fill that need?

And, lo, there it was! We did not have to write anything. We already had it! For several years now, David has traveled regularly and extensively in his work developing a lay ministries program and resurrecting the Men's Program of the Southern Baptist Convention. Somewhere along the way, he fell into the habit of writing notes and letters to me while traveling. Usually these were written on his flight home. Some, however, were written before leaving home and placed under my pillow. How I enjoy those letters!

This book is a selection of those personal letters to me. There is a noticeable lack of advice. They are just letters, actual letters, from a husband, father, and struggler to his wife.

Likewise, there is a noticeable lack of a voice of

"authority." We are still amateurs in this experience of marriage! If twenty-five years together has taught us anything, it is that we don't have *the* answers. The letters in this book are merely a "report" from two veterans of domestic wars.

Thus, we offer *Traveling Together* as our contribution, alongside the sound advice and solid theory of others, as *personal experience*. We pray it will help you. The letters surely helped us!

Aileen F. Haney

There are persons whose names appear regularly in the book. These are—

Karen, our daughter and oldest child

Steve, our son and middle child

Philip, our younger son

Ronny, our son-in-law (Karen's husband)

Wesley, our beloved grandchild

All other names have been changed; in one or two instances, place-names have been changed to avoid embarrassment.

1.   "Ole Dumb Me"

Well, I'm on my way home from Seattle. The conference went well and I enjoyed the time there, but as always I'm glad to be headed home.

Aileen, I like you! Yes, before you ask, I love you, too. But I mean more than that: I *like* you!

What do I like about you? Well, a lot of things.

One of them is your way of laughing at yourself. Does that seem odd to you? Let me explain. In contrast to you, I am so serious and intense about most of what I do that I often overdo it. If I misplace something, for instance, I can't figure it out! I'm so methodical that I *always* put everything "in its place"; and when I can't find something, I begin to blame others ("All right, who's got my pencil?") and myself ("How could I have done that?") until it becomes a trauma.

But not you. You just laugh at yourself ("Ole dumb me") and go on. It doesn't matter what it is, you just take it in stride, never taking yourself too seriously, and chuckle your way through and beyond it. I like that in you.

You've taught me to be more that way, too. Not as much as you, of course, but I'm so much better about it than I was. So you have blessed me twice-over!

Now where is that envelope I was going to put this letter in? "Oh, for crying out loud, Haney, how dumb can you be? Where'd you put it? All right, who's got my . . . ?"

Prayer:

Lord, I thank You for my wife and for her ability to laugh at the "small stuff" of life. I like that in her. Teach me to be that way, too. Maybe You are already doing that—through her. Amen.

Now, Between the Two of You:

1. One of you read the selection above.
2. Share with each other one good thing you like about each other.
3. Read the Bible together. Use Romans 12:3-5.
4. In your prayer together, thank the Father for those good things He has brought into your life through your mate.

Romans 12:3-5:

For by the grace given me I say to every one of you: Do not think of yourself more highly than you ought, but rather think of yourself with sober judgment, in accordance with the measure of faith God has given you. Just as each of us has one body with many members, and these members do not all have the same function, so in Christ we who are many form one body, and each member belongs to all the others.

2. Should This Plane Go Down

I'm on my way home from Tulsa now. It's been a long day. I left home at 9:00 A.M., spent four hours in Dallas with some leaders there, then went on to Tulsa to consult with a church, and now am headed home on the last flight out to Memphis.

I heard about the plane crash today. So many people were killed. I can only imagine what their families are going through tonight. So swiftly their lives have been deprived and unalterably changed.

Yes, I think of airplane crashes from time to time. As much as I travel, I have to be aware of them. I thought today, too, of what effect it would have on us should such a thing happen.

So, as morbid as this may sound, the insurance papers are in the box in our closet, and all the contracts and bills are in the bottom desk drawer. They are all organized (with notes) "just in case."

Do you remember that the very first contract we ever signed was an insurance policy? We were newly married, away at school, and were somewhat below what they now call the "poverty level." (I'm glad they didn't have a name for it then; it would have scared me to death!) But I knew then that we needed to be protected, so I took out that "big" policy. It was for $2000!

Well, I've added to that coverage since, but the feeling is the same. To know that you and the children are taken care of is important to me. So, if something should happen (God forbid), you'll know where to look.

And, should something happen, I want you to know this—if time permits, I go down both praying for and loving you. That abiding sense of love we've shared is far more secure and securing than any insurance policy could ever be.

Well, we just landed. All is well. But I'll give this to you anyway—since I fly to New Orleans day after tomorrow! I love you!

Prayer:

> Lord, thank You for my family and what they mean to me. Yet I know that while they are a blessing to me, they are also a responsibility. Lord, help me to be both responsive and responsible. Amen.

Now, Between the Two of You:

1. One of you read the selection.
2. Discuss with each other:
   a. Where your important papers are.
   b. What the word *security* means to you.
3. Read the Bible together. Use Romans 14:7-9.
4. In your prayer together, ask the Father to help you see your responsibilities to the rest of your family and to meet them.

Romans 14:7-9:

For none of us lives to himself alone and none of us dies to himself alone. If we live, we live to the Lord; and if we die, we die to the Lord. So, whether we live or die, we belong to the Lord.

For this very reason, Christ died and returned to life so that he might be the Lord of both the dead and the living.

3. Life Begins At Forty, "They" Say

So you're forty now. As I left for Atlanta yesterday, the memory of your birthday party the night before was still fresh in my mind.

Did I really surprise you? Well, I tried to. I invited all the guests, ordered the cake, got Karen [our daughter] to help with hosting, and tried to keep it a secret. We drove off that night, "going out" to dinner, arrived there, and I'd "forgotten" my wallet. So we drove back home to get it and—"Happy Birthday!" I wish I had gotten a picture of your face at that very moment!

Did it bother you, turning forty? It didn't bother me last year. Now, thirty did. But not forty. And it shouldn't bother you either.

Why do I say that? For many reasons. One is that, at forty, you are prettier than ever, Aileen. You really are. I know that all the "studies" say that women fear forty, that they begin to fear that they've lost their appeal physically, etc. But not you. I honestly think that you are prettier now than you were at twenty or thirty.

Yes, I know that there are a few more lines in your face, but they are life and living lines. They speak of maturity and experience. I like that. And, yes, I'm aware that some features are shaped differently now, but I see the process as mellowing, not aging, and I like it even better. I never cease to be amazed that you keep on "turning me on."

And others find you attractive, too! Remember the other day in Houston? We were at the airport terminal, ready to catch the bus to the airport. I had gone to get the tickets, and the bus driver saw you alone and began flirting with you. You really are pretty, Aileen.

I love you—and I'm glad I'm coming home to you now.

Prayer:

> Lord, I thank You that love includes the physical, as well as all the other dimensions of personality. And I thank You for giving me the one You did. Thank You for the years we've had together and for the mellowing beauty of both her and the years. Give us many more! Amen.

Now, Between the Two of You:

1. One of you read the selection above.
2. Share with each other:
   a. The time your spouse appeared the prettiest or most handsome to you or to others.
   b. An attractive physical feature of each other.
   c. An attractive spiritual feature of each other.

3. Read the Bible together. Use Philippians 1:3-11.
4. In your prayer together, thank God for the beauty you see in each other and for the beauty of the years you've had together.

Philippians 1:3-11:

I thank my God every time I remember you. In all my prayers for all of you, I always pray with joy because of your partnership in the gospel from the first day until now, being confident of this, that he who began a good work in you will carry it on to completion until the day of Christ Jesus.

It is right for me to feel this way about all of you, since I have you in my heart; for whether I am in chains or defending and confirming the gospel, all of you share in God's grace with me. God can testify how I long for all of you with the affection of Christ Jesus.

And this is my prayer: that your love may abound more and more in knowledge and depth of insight, so that you may be able to discern what is best and may be pure and blameless until the day of Christ, filled with the fruit of righteousness that comes through Jesus Christ—to the glory and praise of God.

4. You Are Really "For Real"

Well, I'm off again. The first of three couples' retreats we are to do this summer is behind us now. And you did just great!

This is the first retreat we've done together in quite a while. I know, with your teaching, you can't get away during the school year, but the summer is a good time for us to do things together.

What I started out to share with you is this: You have grown! I was surprised (and proud) when you stepped up before that group just like a "pro." You were great!

Do you know what you communicate—beyond the words and subject matter? You communicate *authenticity*. You come across as being "real." So many times people put the speaker and his wife on a pedestal and can't identify with them, but you utterly destroy that and get through to them.

As you led the group discussion times, you shared what your answer would be to each question. It was clear enough that they got the idea, and you were *honest* enough to allow them to be honest, too. I've never seen groups open up so quickly, and it can be greatly attributed to your being vulnerable and open first.

After the third session, one couple invited me to have coffee with them while you were talking with another couple. Well, we talked about you! Know what they said?

They said that they *really* liked you. Do you know what they gave as reasons? First, they liked the way you laughed at yourself. You had drawn something on the chalkboard to illustrate the group discussion topics and it didn't look like what you said it was—an airplane, I think—and you just laughed with the rest of us. Then they mentioned how honest you were with them. You had shared something with the group about a failure, and the fact that you could and would share it meant a lot to them.

So, you see, it's not just your husband who thinks you're great. Others do, too!

Prayer:

Lord, I thank You for a growing, ever-new mate. Her gifts, so different from mine, serve to complete and to improve me. Help her grow even more. Help *us* grow more. Amen.

Now, Between the Two of You:

1. One of you read the selection above.
2. Share with each other:
   a. A way or an area in which you have seen each other grow.
   b. Something good someone else has told you about the other.

3. Read the Bible together. Use 1 Thessalonians 1:2-10.

4. In your prayer time, thank the Father for specific areas of growth in each other and ask His help in other specific areas where you personally need to grow.

1 Thessalonians 1:2-10:

We always thank God for all of you, mentioning you in our prayers. We continually remember before our God and Father your work produced by faith, your labor prompted by love, and your endurance inspired by hope in our Lord Jesus Christ.

Brothers loved by God, we know that he has chosen you, because our gospel came to you not simply with words, but also with power, with the Holy Spirit and with deep conviction. You know how we lived among you for your sake. You became imitators of us and of the Lord; in spite of severe suffering, you welcomed the message with the joy given by the Holy Spirit. And so you became a model to all the believers in Macedonia and Achaia. The Lord's message rang out from you not only in Macedonia and Achaia—your faith in God has become known everywhere. Therefore we do not need to say anything about it, for they themselves report what kind of reception you gave us. They tell how you turned to God from idols to serve the living and true God, and to wait for his Son from heaven, whom he raised from the dead—Jesus, who rescues us from the coming wrath.

5. About Family Traditions

Our son Steve's birthday has come and gone. Yesterday was such a happy day!

Do *you* feel older too? It's strange, isn't it, that someone else's birthday can make another person feel older? But when it is one's own child, it can't help but do just that. And, truthfully, we *are* older. The kids are growing up and we've been at this marriage for nearly twenty-two years now. Long enough to have "traditions."

I was thinking about that yesterday as I told Steve of the circumstances of his birth . . . again. He said, "Oh, Dad, not again!" but loved every minute of it. All three children are the same.

When did I start doing that—telling them the stories of their births on their birthdays? I don't remember, but it's been a long time. It has become a "family tradition" now. They expect it.

The other thing which struck me about it is that I didn't set out to *begin* a family tradition. It just grew into one. Maybe a family ought to deliberately create them. Maybe not, but every family ought to have them. Family traditions give a family a sense of continuity, of history, of belonging.

Couples ought to have "traditions," also. Like our

nightly bowl of popcorn together. We've had it whether we even liked each other or not some evenings! Or the way we've said, "I love you," to each other every night before going to sleep. Those sorts of things give continuity and security to our lives—and a lot of happiness, memories, and hopes.

In fact, these "traveling letters" have become a tradition, too. You always anticipate getting one. Sometimes I don't give it to you right away and I can tell you're waiting. Sometimes it's all you can do to keep from asking! I enjoy that.

I like the fact that we've got a history. And all our traditions serve to remind us of segments of that history—happy times, happy memories, brought back to life. And not only that, they give us hope for the *future*, too—and *new* traditions!

Prayer:

> Lord, how many times in the Scriptures are stories of events told and retold. Thank You that You have given us personal stories, too, stories that bear repeating. Grant to us now a future that will bear repeating. Amen.

Now, Between the Two of You:

1. One of you read the selection above.
2. Share with each other:
   a. A family tradition you had while growing up.

  b. A family tradition the two of you have now.
  c. A family tradition you'd like to start.
3. Read the Bible together. Use Philippians 4:8-9.
4. In your prayer time, thank God for specific traditions and the joys they bring to you both.

Philippians 4:8-9:

Finally, brothers, whatever is true, whatever is noble, whatever is right, whatever is pure, whatever is lovely, whatever is admirable—if anything is excellent or praiseworthy—think about such things. Whatever you have learned or received or heard from me, or seen in me—put into practice. And the God of peace will be with you.

6. May I Call You Too?

To be honest, I was a little bothered when I left the other morning. I am going to be gone all week, and I was looking forward to spending the evening with you. But the phone rang—and rang!

After having thought and prayed about it, though, I feel a little better. In fact, I ought to be ashamed. The people who called you needed help and turned to you via the telephone.

I remember Joyce once saying that you were so easy to talk to and that you "never give advice!"

First, Doris called. Her radiation treatments aren't working, at least not as fast as they had hoped. I know you helped her in the midst of a terrible experience.

Then Lynette called from Denver. (I really miss having her and her husband as neighbors.) She and John have separated after fifteen years of marriage. How sad! Yet she too turned to you for what John Drakeford called "the awesome power of the listening ear."

Next, Steve (our son) called from college. Something had happened and he was ready to explode. So he called you. Not me, mind you (maybe I am too quick to "give advice"?), but you.

Finally, Janice called. Her father is ill again, and

she felt as if you were the one to call and to share it with.

By that time, I was already asleep! But you were still up and caring.

So I was upset. "Our" evening was spent by *you* caring for *others!* How selfish of me!

In fact, I'm thinking about calling you myself. You see, I've got this problem with a wife who is always being called on the phone and. . . .

Prayer:

Lord, as One whose time had demands placed upon it by others, help us to give of ourselves to others and to give each other to others, too. Amen.

Now, Between the Two of You:

1. One of you read the selection above.
2. Share with each other:
   a. A way in which you could spend more time with each other.
   b. A way in which you could free each other to give more time in ministry to others, including members of the family.
3. Read the Bible together. Use Matthew 6:33-34.
4. In your prayer time, thank God for the ways your mate ministers to others.

Matthew 6:33-34:

"But seek first his kingdom and his righteousness, and all these things will be given to you as well. Therefore do not worry about tomorrow, for tomorrow will worry about itself. Each day has enough trouble of its own."

7. A Good Mother To All of Us

I'm in Pineville, Louisiana, tonight and will be coming home tomorrow. Louisiana College is here. School is out for the summer, but a few students are still around.

Perhaps Steve would like to be here with his classmates, but he will have to wait until fall. He'll be a sophomore then.

I couldn't help but think what a good mother you are. Steve is such a well-adjusted young man and has a good grasp of his goals.

And in just three weeks Karen will be getting married. Ronny is just the choice of a son-in-law we would have made for her. They, too, are solid young people and have pursued their goals with a determination that makes me proud.

You've been a good mom to Philip, too. He is growing up with that same good balance.

They have all turned out well—no trouble, no "delinquency." And the credit is far more yours than mine. You would never say that, but it's true. They reflect your personality and ways—and I'm glad of that!

If I were in the pulpit, I would call it your "ministry" as a mother, but that is a little sanctimonious for a letter. I'll just say that you've done a terrific job.

You've been a good "mother" to me, too! I remember Keith Miller once saying that every man wants his wife to be a "mother" to him, in some ways—at least until nighttime! Well, you are—just that.

Prayer:

O Lord, the role of a mate is to be spouse, parent, and child to the other. I thank You for each of these in my personal trinity of a mate. Amen.

Now, Between the Two of You:

1. One of you read the selection above.
2. Share with each other:
   a. A time when each has been a "parent" to the other.
   b. An example of how the other has been a good parent to your children, if you have any.
3. Read the Bible together. Use 2 John 4-6.
4. In your prayer time, thank God for specific instances of good parenting to each other and to your children.

2 John 4-6:

It has given me great joy to find some of your children walking in the truth, just as the Father commanded us. And now, dear lady, I am not writing you a new command but one we have had from the beginning. I ask that we love one another. And this is love: that we walk in obedience to his commands. As you have heard from the beginning, his command is that you walk in love.

8. How Much Is "Too Much"?

I've been off again, this time to Ohio, but am headed home.

It's been a good trip, a productive one, I think; but lately you don't seem to think *any* of these trips are that important. You think I'm gone too much.

How much is "too much"? And for whom is it "too much"? For you? For the kids?

That's a part of the turmoil I'm in now and have been in for some time. I don't think you understand, and maybe you are not even trying to.

Here's the dilemma I face, Aileen. I've got a job to do. This program is my assignment, and there is no one else to do it. When a call comes, I've got to go, if for no other reason than the fact that there is no one else to go. At times it really loads up.

Another aspect of it is financial. Sometimes the trips are "personal" speaking engagements, for which I'm paid. And we need the money. I know that sounds mercenary, but it is true. Sometimes I don't think you understand that—or don't believe it! Yet when we need "extra money," this is where I get it! Right now we've got two children in college, one of whom is our daughter who is getting married soon. We've got one going to the orthodontist. The house needs painting. And all of that spells M-O-N-E-Y!

Yet the irony of it—and what hurts most—is that I have to take away from those I love to provide the things which love requires! So how should I do it? I can only try to provide a balance and hope that I can somehow do a good job of both.

When you give me those "looks" as I get ready to leave, it really hurts. Yet I would hurt if I didn't go, too! So, for a little while yet, till college and dentists are over, please be patient.

I know you have a "side" to this, too. Let's talk about it—*before* my *next* trip!

Prayer:

Help us, O Lord, to learn how to resolve our conflicts and to lose our wills and plans in Yours. Amen.

Now, Between the Two of You:

1. One of you read the selection above.
2. Share with each other a past conflict that was happily resolved.
3. Read the Bible together. Use Philippians 1:12-26.
4. In your prayer time, thank God for all His help (past, present, future) in resolving conflicts.

36

Philippians 1:12-26:

Now I want you to know, brothers, that what has happened to me has really served to advance the gospel. As a result, it has become clear throughout the whole palace guard and to everyone else that I am in chains for Christ. Because of my chains, most of the brothers in the Lord have been encouraged to speak the word of God more courageously and fearlessly.

It is true that some preach Christ out of envy and rivalry, but others out of good will. The latter do so in love, knowing that I am put here for the defense of the gospel. The former preach Christ out of selfish ambition, not sincerely, supposing that they can stir up trouble for me while I am in chains. But what does it matter? The important thing is that in every way, whether from false motives or true, Christ is preached. And because of this I rejoice.

Yes, and I will continue to rejoice, for I know that through your prayers and the help given by the Spirit of Jesus Christ, what has happened to me will turn out for my deliverance. I eagerly expect and hope that I will in no way be ashamed, but will have sufficient courage so that now as always Christ will be exalted in my body, whether by life or death. For to me, to live is Christ and to die is gain. If I am to go on living in the body, this will mean fruitful labor for me. Yet what shall I choose? I do not know! I am torn between the two: I desire to depart and be with Christ, which is better by far; but it is more necessary for you that I remain in the body. Convinced of this, I know that I will remain, and I will continue with all of you for your progress and joy in the faith, so that through my being with you again your joy in Christ Jesus will overflow on account of me.

9. Pennies From Heaven

The trip is almost over. It has been a long week here in California, but one of the finest and most rewarding I have ever experienced. We spent the first three days up in the Sequoia Mountains training 300 college students to lead groups. Then we came back to Fresno for the youth conference the past four days. Each of the college students worked with 10 high school students. That's right: we actually had 3000 for the conference! What a celebration it was!

I guess you found that pile of pennies I left on the table. I meant to put them on Philip's desk and forgot. As you know, each night as I empty my pockets, I sort out the pennies for Philip. I did it for Steve, too, before he left for college.

Pennies! Do you remember that time in college when we spent our *last roll* of pennies? We had saved pennies before we were married and had quite a few. Then, after a few months in college, we had spent all our money and had only those rolls of pennies. I remember when we gave that last roll to the paper boy and we were broke!

At the time it didn't seem too serious. I don't recall that it bothered us much. What faith (or foolishness!) we had back then. Today I'd panic!

Poverty is so relative, isn't it? The word *poverty* when used in our country means something different than it would in some other parts of the world, but it is still an ominous word.

Yet we were so rich at the same time, weren't we? We were so young, so naive, so bodacious in our faith, so in love, so excited about life and the future. What else did we need?

And, as I recall, that very week I was contacted by what was to be our first church! Sadieville Baptist Church in Sadieville, Kentucky—what great people they were! From poverty to provision. God always provides.

I just hope Philip discovers that—before he gets down to *his* last roll of pennies!

Prayer:

Lord, thank You for always being the great Provider of both pennies and blessings. Amen.

Now, Between the Two of You:

1. One of you read the selection above.
2. Share with each other a time when each of you has seen the provision of God in a time of a need. Rejoice in it.
3. Read the Bible together. Use Matthew 6:25-32.
4. In your prayer time, thank God for providing for you and for a recent evidence of His blessing.

Matthew 6:25-32:

"Therefore I tell you, do not worry about your life, what you will eat or drink; or about your body, what you will wear. Is not life more important than food, and the body more important than clothes? Look at the birds of the air; they do not sow or reap or store away in barns, yet your heavenly Father feeds them. Are you not much more valuable than they? Who of you by worrying can add a single hour to his life.

And why do you worry about clothes? See how the lilies of the field grow. They do not labor or spin. Yet I tell you that not even Solomon in all his splendor was dressed like one of these. If that is how God clothes the grass of the field, which is here today and tomorrow is thrown into the fire, will he not much more clothe you, O you of little faith? So do not worry, saying, 'What shall we eat?' or 'What shall we drink?' or 'What shall we wear?' For the pagans run after all these things, and your heavenly Father knows that you need them."

10. A Minor Case of Jealousy

It was good to talk with you tonight, although the telephone is a poor substitute for being together. The stars are out all over the Alabama sky tonight—I wish you were *here!*

So Jim called you again tonight. . . . Well, I'm glad we can joke about it. He certainly knows my schedule and when I'm out of town, doesn't he? Sometimes I think he knows it better than I do!

I wonder what makes him think that you are (or would be) interested in going out with him? I know he and Patricia have a difficult marriage (or so he says), but to believe that breaking into another's marriage is the cure "bends" the seventh commandment a little!

I suspect that it has to do with your ability to listen. When he first started calling, it was for help, a sympathetic ear, a shoulder to cry on, and a listening friend. Maybe he has confused your concern for him with a physical attraction. I don't know. But whatever it is, he has a bad case of it!

Am I jealous? Not really, not in his case anyway. Rather, I feel sorry for him.

I was reading the other day in a journal about the different kinds of jealousy. There is one type that is an all-inclusive, *possessive* jealousy. Then there is a *selective* jealousy which is for specific persons and times. I suppose that my jealousy is more the selective kind, and he isn't one of "the select."

What can we do to help? Shoud *we* talk with him? Should *you* talk to him? Should *I?* Let's discuss the possibilities when I get back on Thursday. In the meantime, let's pray that God will use us in a redemptive way.

Prayer:

Thank You, Lord, for a mate to love and whose love is worth sharing. Amen.

Now, Between the Two of You:

1. One of you read the selection above.
2. Share with each other regarding the difference in *possessive* and *selective* jealousy and how it relates to each of you.
3. Read the Bible together. Use Matthew 6:14-15.
4. In your prayer time, thank the Father for the genuine love you have for each other.

Matthew 6:14-15:

"For if you forgive men when they sin against you, your heavenly Father will also forgive you. But if you do not forgive men their sins, your Father will not forgive your sins."

11. My Goals—Your Goals —Our Goals

Well, I'm finally headed home—to the good old U.S.A. Australia and New Zealand are beautiful, and my conferences were well received, but after four weeks I've had enough. I'm on the island of Fiji for two days and then on to Memphis.

My trip here has been the realization of a goal for me: to preach and teach and learn "down under." To have done it is a *satisfying* feeling. It gives me a sense of fulfillment, of completion or wholeness.

And now, on to the next goal!

But what about *your* goals? I have to be honest and tell you that there was a time when I thought you didn't have any goals. I honestly (and sadly) believed that all of your goals were tied to mine—that the purpose of your existence was to help me reach *my* goals!

When did I see the truth? I don't remember. It was a slow "dawning upon," I guess. But I began to see it and share it with you and, lo and behold, you were thinking the same thing! What a revelation it was to both of us. That God has *created* you and *gifted* you for specific things; that your *wholeness* depended upon the discovery and use of your gifts; and that a part of my ministry was to help you accomplish this—wow!

I admit to having some struggles with your becoming your own person. And it has brought significant changes. You went back to school, got your degree (with "honors," no less), and now are teaching school—just what God created and gifted you to do. And, wonder of wonders, you're even a better wife. God sure knows what He's doing, doesn't He?

Prayer:

O Lord, thank You for showing us, again and again, that Your will is satisfying and always just right for both of us. Amen.

Now, Between the Two of You:

1. One of you read the selection above.
2. Share with each other:
   a. Goals which have been attained by the two of you.
   b. Goals which have changed over the years.
   c. Some new goals, both personal and as a couple.
3. Read the Bible together. Use Ephesians 3:14-19.
4. In your prayer, thank God for the achievements of the past and the gift of new ones.

Ephesians 3:14-19:

For this reason I kneel before the Father, from whom his whole family in heaven and on earth derives its name. I pray that out of his glorious riches he may strengthen you with power through his Spirit in your inner being, so that Christ may dwell in your hearts through faith. And I pray that you, being rooted and established in love, may have power, together with all the saints, to grasp how wide and long and high and deep is the love of Christ, and to know this love that surpasses knowledge—that you may be filled to the measure of all the fullness of God.

12. Is This Your Honeymoon?

It was a rough flight from Memphis to Indianapolis, but we made it. The Baptist World Alliance Men's Meeting is going well. I have two sessions per day and I'm enjoying them.

Indianapolis! I have a lot of memories of the city. When I was young, our family used to visit here. My Uncle Sam and Aunt Margie live here (I'm going to see them tomorrow night), and we used to drive over from Dayton to see them in the summer.

Then, as a teenager I used to come here to the "Indy 500" for the time trials and races. Back then my ambition was to be a race-car driver (remember?), and I drove over here in that 1938 Plymouth with the "souped-up" engine just as if Route 40 were the straightaway!

But the thing I remember most about Indianapolis was that day you and I spent here on vacation. Remember?

We had decided to take a "swimming vacation." It was to be our first vacation away from the kids, and we were going to drive a hundred miles or so each day, then stop at a motel with a pool and swim the rest of the day. Indianapolis was our first stop.

What I recall about Indianapolis on that trip was

the question of the lady at the motel. I'll bet you've forgotten! It was a "Mom and Pop" motel. We had been swimming and playing in the pool—waterfights and so on—when I went back to the room for something and "Mom" asked you if we were on our honeymoon! How we laughed when you told me later. We had been married over five years and had two children by then, but we were so pleased that we could be taken as being "honeymooners."

We've not lost that playful part of our marriage yet, not even after all these years! The truth is, I still *enjoy* you. Now that our children are growing up and leaving, I'm looking forward to the time when it will be just the two of us again. Maybe it will be like "vacation" *all* the time!

Prayer:

Lord, Thank You for the times of playfulness which love affords us. Keep us ever in the playful mood. Amen.

Now, Between the Two of You:

1. One of you read the selection above.
2. Share a particularly happy and playful time you remember together.
3. Read the Bible together. Use Matthew 18:1-3.
4. In your prayer time, thank God for the "child" in your mate.

Matthew 18:1-3:

> At that time the disciples came to Jesus and asked,
> "Who is the greatest in the kingdom of heaven?"
>   He called a little child and had him stand among
> them. And he said: "I tell you the truth, unless you
> change and become like little children, you will
> never enter the kingdom of heaven."

13. Relaxed and Proud

Hello from Nashville! This is the first meeting of the Baptist Medical-Dental Fellowship that you have missed, and I wish you were here.

Tonight they officially called their first full-time executive director, so my work as the "volunteer" director is over. I've enjoyed it.

It was four years ago that the small group of physicians and dentists asked me to help them get organized. Because of my work in lay ministries, they felt I would be interested. Was I ever! To think that a group of physicians and dentists would want to organize a fellowship designed to promote volunteer mission service overseas and at home was—and is—exciting! And from that group to this: tonight they announced their mailing list now has over 4000 names on it! They gave reports of mission service in Yemen, Nigeria, on Indian reservations, in free clinics in their hometowns, and on and on. It was a great time. You ought to have been here.

I remember that second year, the year it met in Orlando, when you were with me. Of all the trips we've taken together, that one stands out among the best for two reasons.

First, during that meeting I spoke to the group, and

after I finished and returned to sit beside you, there was a gleam in your eye and you said, "I'm proud of you." That really registered with me. After all those years, you were still proud of me!

Second, we slipped away one afternoon and went to a flea market that encircled the lake in downtown Orlando. It was such a relaxed time, and we just wandered about taking in the beauty of the place and looking at all the things for sale. Those relaxed times are so scarce that I guess it just engraved itself on my mind. We need to have more of them!

Prayer:

Lord, how we long for the approval and pleasure of those whose approval and pleasure mean the most. Thank You for providing it through those who love us. Amen.

Now, Between the Two of You:

1. One of you read the selection above.
2. Share with each other a time when each of you strongly felt the approval of each other.
3. Read the Bible together. Use Matthew 25:21.
4. In your prayer time, confess your need for approval from each other and ask God's help in making you both better "approvers."

Matthew 25:21:

*"His master replied, 'Well done, good and faithful
servant! You have been faithful with a few things; I
will put you in charge of many things. Come and
share your master's happiness!'"*

14.   The Little Woman

The convention is going well and my sessions are too. I'll be home shortly.

I came away from the session this afternoon somewhat frustrated, however. The featured speaker was to deal with "the family" and he really did a number on it. It was more a protest against his perception of the "drift of family life in our country" (though I think it was more like his *county*) and how it could be traced to just one source: *women out of their place!* That "place," according to him, is the circuit which covers the kitchen, the bedroom, the grocery store, and the P.T.A. His shoddy thinking was surpassed only by his lousy theology.

After the session, all the speakers went out for dinner and I got to talk with him. At least he is married. (So many of these "family experts" are not, you know.) But his conversation was dotted with words and phrases such as, "the little woman," "my old lady," men "taking charge," and the like. You'd have been proud of me. I kept my cool . . . for once!

Aside from the faulty exegesis and warped psychology, how can such men demean God's creation so? It is as though they believe that God only gave dreams and goals and abilities and gifts to *men*. Yet God gives them to women, too. And if that were the case, He surely overendowed women if they are "only" to fix dinners and rear children!

I'm sure that speaker would say that I've been influenced by the women's movement. Not really. Just the New Testament.

And you!

Prayer:

O Lord, Giver of life and dreams, thank You for giving both life and dreams to both of us. Help us to merge them more perfectly in Your will. Amen.

Now, Between the Two of You:

1. One of you read the selection above.
2. Share with each other your dreams for each other.
3. Read the Bible together. Use Galations 3:28
4. In your prayer together, thank God for the gifts He has given to each of you and ask for His help in furthering their implementation.

Galatians 3:28:

There is neither Jew nor Greek, slave nor free, male nor female, for you are all one in Christ Jesus.

15. Sightseeing Alone

Hello from Mexico City! I spoke last night and will again tonight, then back to the homefires. Quick trip.

I'm free until tonight, so I slept late, had breakfast, and thought I'd go sightseeing. My hotel is near the center of the city, so I am close to many things to see.

There is a beautiful park in the center of town with lots of flowers, historical markers, and statuary. Several museums are close, too. It was interesting, but it is so different to sightsee *alone!* You need to be here, too!

When a person goes sightseeing, he needs someone beside him to nudge and say, "Look at this." It is a part of *sharing* life, I guess.

You have never had the experience of being alone in some distant place, have you? Well, if you were, where would you like for it to be?

In fact, where would *you* like to go *together?* It seems as if I am the one who always suggests places to go. Where would *you* like to go . . . and take me along?

My favorite places, those I would like to go back to and take you (where you have never been), are Fiji in the South Pacific and Caracas, Venezuela. The places where we have been together and where I'd like to return are the Swiss Alps and Kelly's Island in Lake Erie.

What about you? Where would you like to go and to take me? Let me guess: Hawaii? New England in autumn? London? As for places we've been, I'd guess you'd like to go back to Holland. Am I right?

I'll tell you what: *You* plan our next vacation, OK?

Prayer:

> O Lord, You are both a sight-creating and sightseeing God. To each step of creation, You looked and spoke of it with enjoyment. Help us to see Your sights and, in them, to see You more clearly. Amen.

Now, Between the Two of You:

1. One of you read the selection above.
2. Share with each other those places:
   a. You would like to take each other.
   b. You would like to return to and see again.
3. Read the Bible together. Use John 1:35-39.
4. In your prayer together, thank God for the privilege and joy of sharing sights as well as seeing them.

John 1:35-39:

> *The next day John was there again with two of his disciples. When he saw Jesus passing by, he said,*

55

"*Look, the Lamb of God!*"

When the two disciples heard him say this, they followed Jesus. Turning around, Jesus saw them following and asked, "*What do you want?*"

They said, "*Rabbi*" (which means Teacher), "*where are you staying?*"

"*Come,*" he replied, "*and you will see.*"

So they went and saw where he was staying, and spent that day with him. It was about the tenth hour.

16.   And Now, a Grandmother!

This is my first letter to you as . . . grandmother! Congratulations! Wesley David Russell was born September 2.

The three days I was able to see him, before I left for Pennsylvania, were a treat. I wish I could be there with you now.

You will make a wonderful grandmother; I know that. But, me a *grandfather?* I can't believe it! But it is true, and I'm glad.

What kind of grandfather will I be? Well, I have several role-models from which to choose and borrow.

My Grandfather Haney, the old country veterinarian, was one such model. Ramrod straight till the day he died, lean and strong, he was always telling us stories. When we went to his house, he gathered us kids around him and began to tell his "tall tales," most of which were far-fetched and unbelievable, sometimes scary and sometimes funny, but we loved every one of them and loved him dearly.

My Grandfather Bales, on the other hand, was the serious saint. A patriarch to his family ("unto the third generation"), he seldom spoke, but when he did it was "the wisdom of the ages." I always thought that God must have sounded like Grandpa Bales! He was a tower of strength to all who knew him, but especially to us grandchildren. When we needed advice, there was never a question as to whom to turn.

My own father—how he loved our children, his grandchildren! He was always holding them, laughing with them, getting down on the floor with them, buying them new toys—a giver.

And I think of your dad, too. He treated every child like an adult. When he talked to the children, asked them questions, and took them for walks, they all felt like "grown-ups" because he took them so seriously.

One by one, these men have gone on, passed away. But I'm heir and beneficiary of each of them. Could I choose, I would like to be a little of each of them to Wes. (I've already nicknamed him!) I'd like for him to look forward to seeing me, as I did Grandpa Haney; to feel free to play with me as our kids did with dad; to know I'm taking him seriously as did your dad with his grandchildren; and to see God the Father in me as I did in Grandpa Bales. All of that—and more—is my "grandfather's prayer."

I know you are having similar thoughts, too, back in Memphis. And I know this—you'll be the best grandmother ever! And, why not? He's the best grandchild ever, isn't he?

Prayer:

Thank You, Father, for allowing us not only the joy of life, but also of producing new life.

Thank You for the supreme joy of seeing that
life go on even unto grandchildren. Amen.

Now, Between the Two of You:

1. One of you read the selection above.
2. Share with each other:
   a. Your memories of role-models in your
      grandparents.
   b. Your aspirations as grandparents.
3. Read the Bible together. Use 2 Timothy
   1:3-5.
4. In your prayer together, thank God for all
   the privileges of parenthood and ask for His
   help in all the responsibilities of it.

2 Timothy 1:3-5:

*I thank God, whom I serve, as my forefathers did,
with a clear conscience, as night and day I con-
stantly remember you in my prayers. Recalling your
tears, I long to see you, so that I may be filled with
joy. I have been reminded of your sincere faith,
which first lived in your grandmother Lois and in
your mother Eunice and, I am persuaded, now lives
in you also.*

17. The Nearest Thing to God's Love

Hello from Baton Rouge! It is really nice here—so pretty, so aristocratic. The evangelism conference is going well.

We were here once before—do you remember? It was nearly twenty years ago, and I was leading a revival. I recall how hot and humid it was.

Before I left the other day, I was digging around in the bureau drawers looking for something, when I came across that bundle of notes the kids wrote when they were little. I started reading them and almost was late for the flight!

The one that really got me was one of Karen's. I laughed till I cried. She was about seven or eight, I guess, and was really upset with you. The note read: "Dear Mom, I hate you. Love, Karen." It's still funny after all these years! (Now that Karen has her own child, maybe she'll get one just like it, too!)

But the truth is that you really are lovable—even when I am angry with you! You are so difficult to be upset with for very long.

Why? Because of your obviously transparent love for every one of us. The nearest thing to God's love has to be a mother's love. If His love is like yours, God truly is Love.

Prayer:

O Lord, You too must rejoice in the ways and acts of Your children. Thank You for allowing me to enjoy my children as You do. Amen.

Now, Between the Two of You:

1. One of you read the selection above.
2. Share with each other:
   a. Those funny experiences and incidents from the lives of your children.
   b. How would you describe the "love of God"?
3. Read the Bible together. Use Isaiah 66:13-14.
4. In your prayer together, thank God for His matchless love and for those whose love comes close to it.

Isaiah 66:13-14:

"As a mother comforts her child,
  so will I comfort you;
  and you will be comforted over Jerusalem."
When you see this, your heart will rejoice
  and you will flourish like grass;
the hand of the Lord will be made known to his
     servants,
  but his fury will be shown to his foes.

18. "Piggyback" Leadership

Do you believe in the "leadership of the Lord"? I know you do, but how does one *recognize* it when it comes?

I called Bill Bangham today before I left. As you know, the *World Mission Journal* is in bad shape. Circulation has dropped over the past eight years and with both editors gone, we need a pair of men who can "pull it out." With Mike coming, the editor's position is filled. But I've been stumped on the associate editor.

For some reason, Bill's name came to mind during my devotions this morning. He is a natural for it! Why hadn't I thought of him before?

So I called him and asked if he would consider it. He said, "Dianne and I have been discussing it, and I was going to call you today to see if you would consider *me* for the position." Case closed.

He shared Dianne's openness to their move from Annapolis to Memphis, but also her reluctance to leave her parents and sister who live nearby.

"How will she know?" I asked. Bill said that they were committed to doing the Lord's will, and with that sort of openness it would be no problem to her.

Since talking with him and coming on to Little

Rock, I've given that a lot of thought. I remember all the moves we made in those early years—and how you simply "piggybacked" on *my* knowing the Lord's will for *our* lives.

That is, when we went to North Carolina to seminary, to Ohio to take the New Lebanon church, and even when we went to College Avenue Church in Annapolis, *I* felt it was the Lord's will for *my* life, and you simply "went along" with *me.*

When we moved to Memphis, it was a little different. You said you "wanted to pray about it, too." How good that was, how *healthy*—for both of us—that we both saw that God had a plan for each of us.

What had happened in those six years? Why the difference in *our* approach to assessing the Lord's leadership for *our* lives? A key to it was (and is) the recognition that God has a plan for *your* life, too—a recognition by you and, moreso, by me.

I hope Bill and Dianne have come to see that, too!

Prayer:

> Thank You, Lord, for having plans, *big* plans, for us and for the joy of mutually discovering how Your plans for us converge. Amen.

Now, Between the Two of You:

1. One of you read the selection above.
2. Share with each other:
   a. How do you "know" when God is leading you?

      b. How do you "know" when God is lead-
          ing *both* of you?
3. Read the Bible together. Use Psalm 40:7-8.
4. In your prayer time, confess your desire and
    need to know God's perfect will for both of
    your lives.

Psalm 40:7-8:

*Then I said, "Here I am, I have come—
    it is written about me in the scroll.
To do your will, O my God, is my desire;
    your law is within my heart."*

19. In Case of Illness, Call Mommy

Today's letter is from Christchurch, probably the most beautiful city in New Zealand. Someday I'd like to bring you here.

We go on from here to Dunedin, then back to Wellington and on to Auckland. It's going to be busy, but the people here are so responsive. I'm glad I'm here! But I miss you, too.

Last night I *really* missed you. Why? I got sick! I had a late meal, and apparently I got hold of something that got hold of me—it didn't agree with me. About 1:00 A.M. I was really *sick.*

Do you know what it is like to be over 15,000 miles from home, alone, in a motel room, in the middle of the night—and *sick?*

I know you'll say that when I'm sick I want my "mommy." Well, it's true. When I'm sick, I want you right there beside me twenty-four hours a day, holding my hand. Isn't that silly?

You are just the opposite. When you are ill, you want to be left alone. But when I'm sick, I want the whole world to suffer with me! I especially want *you* there.

And you always are. You instantly become the "mother." You "ooh" and "aah" with me, get me this and that, and see to it that I enjoy every minute of being sick!

All of which is to say, "I surely missed you last night, 'Mommy'!"

Prayer:

> Thank You, Lord, for being the Great Physician and for having those who help You, too! Amen.

Now, Between the Two of You:

1. One of you read the selection above.
2. Share with each other:
   a. When you are sick, do you want a "mate" or a "mother" to help you?
   b. Who would you most like to have by your side in illness? Why?
3. Read the Bible together. Use Matthew 25:37-40.
4. In your prayer together, thank God for those who care for us when we are in physical need or pain.

Matthew 25:37-40:

> *"Then the righteous will answer him, 'Lord, when did we see you hungry and feed you, or thirsty and give you something to drink? When did we see you a stranger and invite you in, or needing clothes and*

clothe you? When did we see you sick or in prison
and go to visit you?'

   "The King will reply, 'I tell you the truth, whatever you did for one of the least of these brothers of
mine, you did for me.'"

20. Describing a Marriage

Hello from Music City! I'm in Nashville for the seminar and enjoying it. I wish you were here because it is the sort of meeting you so thoroughly enjoy.

I rode up here with Ralph, and it was interesting, to say the least. No sooner had we gotten on the road (at 5:00 A.M.!) than the conversation turned to his wife, Nora.

He obviously needed to talk, because it just seemed to erupt from him with no introduction. He said that things were "a little shaky" and he was glad to get away. After thirty-some years of her hypochondria, of living with her parents or their living with Jack and her (they've never been alone), and of her jealousy of his secretaries, he was just "resigned" to living out the rest of their years with it all, he said.

I tried to be a good listener, and I think it helped—just to listen and not to comment.

As I've reflected over it since, what struck me most was his terminology. When he spoke of his marriage, he used words and phrases like "stuck," "accepted it," "keep peace," "grit my teeth and bear it," and one scary statement about "having to find other outlets" (which he didn't explain and I didn't probe). What terms for a relationship!

What causes a marriage to degenerate like that? I don't know, but I do know this: I thank God for you and whatever it is that keeps me from having to think things like that about us! (Now, I admit there have been instances where I've "gritted my teeth," but. . .)

As I've wondered and prayed over it, I came to a question (not a solution or an answer): Does something like this happen because of something which is done or because of something which isn't done in the relationship? Is it omission or commission—or both?

Whichever—let's keep on doing whatever it is we're doing and keep on refraining from whatever it is we're not doing!

What a difference in "the best is yet to be" and "the best that never was"!

Prayer:

O Lord, thank You for a marriage that is growing with the promise of the best which is always yet to be. Amen.

Now, Between the Two of You:

1. One of you read the selection above.
2. Share with each other the values of growing through open communication.
3. Read the Bible together. Use Ruth 1:16-17.
4. In your prayer together, thank God for the potential of tomorrow together.

Ruth 1:16-17:

> But Ruth replied, "Don't urge me to leave you or to turn back from you. Where you go I will go, and where you stay I will stay. Your people will be my people and your God my God. Where you die I will die, and there I will be buried. May the LORD deal with me, be it ever so severely, if anything but death separates you and me."

21. What Makes the Difference?

I'm in my room in Knoxville after the planning session for the Church Renewal Conference you and I are to participate in this fall. It was a good meeting, and I believe we are off to a good start.

These have been busy days! From Steve's graduation at Louisiana College in Pineville, back to Memphis, and on to Knoxville—all in a week's time!

It was a magnificent experience to be at Steve's graduation. I was so proud—and you were, too. His four years there were significant: a double major (religion and business), named to *Who's Who Among Students in American Colleges and Universities*, student government officer, and all the other awards.

I could not help but compare it with the telephone call which came the day before we left. Kerry Curtiss—the same age as Steve, one of his childhood playmates back East—arrested for the second time for selling drugs!

What makes the difference, Aileen? Kerry was reared in the church; his father is a staff member of a religious organization; his mother is a teacher—just like us! Yet one child turns out good, the other in trouble. One is going on to seminary, the other to jail. Why?

Is it something parents do, or fail to do, that causes or contributes to the situation? Is it something which happens in the early years of training? Or is it something in the child and not the parents?

While I think I know at least part of it in Kerry's situation (we've discussed some of the neglect he's had over the years), I have to admit that there is no universal answer. Sometimes poor parents have good children, and sometimes good parents have difficult children.

Were we just "lucky"?

Whatever it is, I praise God for Steve and share the grief over Kerry. And I praise you, too. Proverbs 31:29 says, "Many women have done excellently, but you surpass them all" (RSV).

I don't know what the answer is, but I'm proud and thankful and humbled, too—for I know how little I had to do with it. The credit belongs to you and the Lord!

Prayer:

> We pray, O Lord, for all children, but uniquely for our own. They are Yours first; help us to rear them as such. Amen.

Now, Between the Two of You:

1. One of you read the selection above.
2. Share with each other the burden of those whose children are having difficulty and dis-

cuss ways of ministering to both the parents and the child.

3. Read the Bible together. Use Proverbs 31:27-31.
4. Thank God for His help in child-rearing and ask for yet more.

Proverbs 31:27-31:

She watches over the affairs of her household
and does not eat the bread of idleness.
Her children arise and call her blessed;
her husband also, and he praises her:
"Many women do noble things, but you surpass
them all."

Charm is deceptive, and beauty is fleeting;
but a woman who fears the LORD *is to be praised.*
Give her the reward she has earned,
and let her works bring her praise at the city gate.

(RSV)

22. Our Daughter: Cancer!

This is a different kind of letter. And it is *by far* the most difficult I've written to you.

Sitting here alone in the Intensive Care waiting room while you've gone to get something to eat, I thought I'd try to express some of the feelings which have been running zigzag patterns through my broken heart and bewildered mind. I doubt that this will make sense even to me, let alone to you.

How did this all begin? Karen had her regular physical examination on Friday. Something appeared on the x-rays that her doctor wanted to "check into." Karen entered the hospital on Monday for additional x-rays and a CAT scan. Tuesday, just before noon, she called me, sobbing, "Dad, it's cancer."

I've been reeling ever since. It's been a week I'd never want to relive.

My first reaction was *anger*. Angry with *whom?* God? The doctor? I don't know. But it was like an explosion within me. It's so *unfair*. Karen is only twenty-three; she and Ronny have so much going for them; and their little Wesley is only nineteen months old. They had planned to have a second child soon—and now this. *Why?*

Grief came on the heels of my anger. I cried—for the very same reasons I was angry!

I've been optimistic and, then, almost simultaneously depressed and hopeless. I've cursed and praised God in the same breath. I've wondered, "Why me?" Yet it is not me, but Karen—who is a part of me.

One thought I've had (that I'm almost afraid to share) is this: I think I could handle this situation better if the victim were myself or even you, my wife, than Karen, our daughter. I don't say this because of any less love for you.

Is it her age, only twenty-three—over against our ages—or the fact that she is a young parent?

Is it the different kind of relationship (and love) that exists between mate and mate than between parent and child?

I don't know. I just know that I hurt.*

Prayer:

Lord, when the pain is so real, be so near. Amen.

Now, Between the Two of You:

1. One of you read the selection above.
2. Share with each other a time when God comforted you in the midst of a trial of faith.
3. Read the Bible together. Use Psalm 42:11.
4. In your prayer together, thank God that even when you question His ways, you still know His love.

Psalm 42:11:

> *Why are you downcast, O my soul?*
>> *Why so disturbed within me?*
> *Put your hope in God,*
>> *for I will yet praise him,*
>> *my Savior and my God.*

*Karen Haney Russell died August 22, 1983, after an eighteen-month battle with cancer. She was twenty-four years old.

23. You and the Computer

As I write this, I am midway into a week of one-day conferences throughout Illinois. The meetings are going well and, while the crowds aren't as large as I'd like, they are responsive.

While I am here, you are leading a seminar, also. I am really proud. Out of all the teachers in the city school system, *you* were asked to lead the math conference for the teachers' association.

Why you? Because you alone saw the value of teaching elementary math with computers! You went out and learned about computers—how to operate them, how to program them—and then developed your own sixth-grade math program.

I know you were scared about doing the four-hour conference this week and I hate to have to be away, but I know you can handle it. I have confidence in you!

Do you remember what I told you about my conversation with Larry before I left? I said to him that I wished he had as much confidence in himself as all of the rest of us had in him. I say it to you as well!

The most difficult step of leading that conference was taken a long time ago. It is past, not present, or future! It was taken when you "followed the dream" and took the first step to find out about computers.

Now that was courage! To lead the seminar? A piece of cake!

Prayer:

O Lord, Giver of strength and courage, grant us both renewed courage to face and conquer life in Your power. Amen.

Now, Between the Two of You:

1. One of you read the selection above.
2. Share with eath other:
   a. A step your mate took which required a step of courage.
   b. A step of courage you took together.
3. Read the Bible together. Use Philippians 4:10-13.
4. In your prayer together, pray for renewed courage to take new steps of faith.

Philippians 4:10-13:

I rejoice greatly in the Lord that at last you have renewed your concern for me. Indeed, you have been concerned, but you had no opportunity to show it. I am not saying this because I am in need, for I have learned to be content whatever the circumstances. I know what it is to be in need, and I know what it is to have plenty. I have learned the secret of being content in any and every situation, whether well fed or hungry, whether living in plenty or in want. I can do everything through him who gives me strength.

24. The Next Twenty Years

On the flight out here, I was reading a book by Carl Rogers in which he discusses what he calls an "actualizing tendency." To illustrate, he tells of how they used to store potatoes at his boyhood home. The potatoes were stored each winter in a bin several feet below a small basement window. Even in that unfavorable situation, the potatoes would begin to sprout! They weren't healthy sprouts—they were pale and spindly—but they were trying to grow. They would never fulfill their potential, but even in the worst of conditions, they were *trying to become.* There is in all of creation that "actualizing tendency" toward growth and fulfillment.

That, coupled with my forthcoming birthday, made me aware that there is an "actualizing tendency" in *me.* It is a drive to grow, to develop, to fulfill that which I am intended to be . . . to *count* for something. Call it "the desire to become" (or whatever), I know that there is more in me and more to me than what is now seen—by me or anyone else.

Both of us are nearing a "milestone," that milestone of "middle age." For all practical purposes, if the age of sixy-five is a relevant terminal point, I have about twenty years left to *count.* You do too.

What should we do with these next twenty years? I don't have a "fix" on mine, but I do have a concern, which may be a clue. It has to do with the many persons who are living such "gray" lives. There are so many who have no obvious purpose, no goals nor ambitions; they are neither black nor white, just gray. And there is so *much more* to life and in life for them. Maybe that's where I need "to count."

And what about you? There is so much more to you and in you, wellsprings that haven't been tapped, depths which haven't been plumbed, areas that haven't been explored. You touch many lives now, but others need to have the benefit of you, too. I want you to think about it.

Finally, I want to count for you, in these next twenty years, more than I have. I want to be more of an encourager, more of an enabler. I want you "to become," and I want to be a part of it. If you'll do the same for me, there is no telling what might happen!

Prayer:

O Lord, thank You that there is more to me than others or I can see, but which You can see. Help me to become more like You and more like the Me You want me to be. Amen.

Now, Between the Two of You:

1. One of you read the selection above.
2. Share with each other some dreams and burdens for your next twenty years.

3. Read the Bible together. Use Philippians 3:12-14.
4. In your prayer together, thank God for His plans for your lives and ask for the grace and wisdom to know how to become.

Philippians 3:12-14:

Not that I have already obtained all this, or have already been made perfect, but I press on to take hold of that for which Christ Jesus took hold of me. Brothers, I do not consider myself yet to have taken hold of it. But one thing I do: Forgetting what is behind and straining toward what is ahead, I press on toward the goal to win the prize for which God has called me heavenward in Christ Jesus.

25. About Companionship

This Sunday is an anniversary for us, and I'll bet you don't know what it is. Give up?

It will be the seventh anniversary of our being co-teachers of our Sunday school class at church. That's right, seven years ago this Sunday we started it.

While it has been a blessing to see it grow from that group of five, to have it divided into new classes year after year, the greatest blessing has been that we've been able to do it *together!*

After all those years that I served as a pastor, when there was so little we could do together, our coming to Memphis and taking the denominational position finally allowed it.

You know, in all those years before that time I'd never heard you teach! I'd heard you give devotions at women's meetings and such, but I'd never really heard the fruits of your study in the Bible. And, to be honest, I was surprised at how good you are at it!

From that, we've gone on to develop a couples' retreat ministry together, leading other kinds of retreats and Lay Renewal weekends, too. A whole new world . . . together!

Just think if I'd stayed in the pastorate—we might

never have discovered the complementary gifts we have!

I enjoy doing things with you. Well, *most* things, that is. (Let's forget grocery shopping, OK?) It's been a growing experience, hasn't it? Marriage is a "growing into" of companionship, and I'm really enjoying it!

Prayer:

For the beauty of life and the beauty of seeing it emerge, thank You, Lord. Amen.

Now, Between the Two of You:

1. One of you read the selection above.
2. Share with each other:
   a. Something beautiful each of you have seen emerge in the other since marriage.
   b. Something new you have begun to do together in recent months or something you would like to do together.
3. Read the Bible together. Use Acts 18:1-4.
4. In your prayer together, pray for one another to more fully "become" and for the beauty of becoming together.

Acts 18:1-4:

After this, Paul left Athens and went to Corinth. There he met a Jew named Aquila, a native of Pontus, who had recently come from Italy with his wife Priscilla, because Claudius had ordered all the Jews to leave Rome. Paul went to see them, and because he was a tentmaker as they were, he stayed and worked with them. Every Sabbath he reasoned in the synagogue, trying to persuade Jews and Greeks.

26. Your Mother and the Nursing Home

I am at mother's house today. She has gone to the office, and I've got a few things to do before heading for Columbus. Dayton looks much the same as before, and it is good to be here.

Last night I stopped by and spent some time with your mother. We had a good visit. I wish I could say she is doing better, but I can't, though she isn't any worse. The Parkinson's is slowly taking its toll on her. It is sad.

How much in contrast are our two mothers. They are the same age, but there is such a radical difference in their health: mine, twice retired and working at yet another job, and yours, so stooped and failing.

I know that one of the most difficult responsibilities you have ever had, if not *the* most difficult, was to put her into the care of a nursing home. I've never seen anything devastate you so, and I felt (and still feel) so helpless to walk that valley with you.

Yet there was no alternative, and I pray that you both know and feel that. I believe you *know* it: she is beyond the point where we could minister to her with the around-the-clock care she requires. But to *feel* it is quite another aspect.

If there is any residue of guilt, I want to affirm you

in the decision. It was the *loving* thing to do, an act of love, not of rejection or dereliction of duty. It was not a case of neglect, or putting her away in an "old folks' home" and forgetting her. Rather, you acted out of a love which wanted the very best care for her. And sometimes love like that *costs*, not money, but the pain of separation.

As I have so often said, "The opposite of love is not hate, but selfishness." To have kept her with us (or rather, to have *tried* to keep her) would have been selfish. Yet so many times people twist such a selfless act of love into a false sense of guilt. You did the right thing, Aileen. Don't ever doubt that. Indeed, if I felt you had not done the right thing, I would have said so. I love your mother too!

Prayer:

> Teach us, O Lord, to act with responsible love toward those who loved us long before we knew the word, let alone its meaning. Amen.

Now, Between the Two of You:

1. One of you read the selection above.
2. Share with each other the requirements of love toward your parents.
3. Read the Bible together. Use John 14:25-27.
4. In your prayer together, pray for guidance to know how to lovingly relate to your parents.

John 14:25-27:

> *"All this I have spoken while still with you. But the Counselor, the Holy Spirit, whom the Father will send in my name, will teach you all things and will remind you of everything I have said to you. Peace I leave with you; my peace I give you. I do not give to you as the world gives. Do not let your hearts be troubled and do not be afraid."*

27. Of Pain and Closeness

For some reason, I'm humming to myself Willie Nelson's song "On the Road Again" a lot these days! It seems like the airport is my "home away from home."

I'm in New Orleans leading the weekend "Koinonia Konference," and from here I go on to Houston to do a management seminar. Busy, busy, busy.

As I sat in the hospital waiting room the other night, I saw something profound taking place. In fact, I'm sharing it this weekend as I preach and teach about "fellowship" (*koinonia*) in the church.

As Karen underwent her chemotherapy treatment (which takes five long days every month) and I was sitting in the "cancer floor" waiting room, I saw something beautiful—and something the church needs to experience, too.

The twenty or so people in that room were strangers to me and to each other, each waiting and hurting and concerned about his or her "Karen"—a parent, mate, child, mother, or sister. Yet there was—how can I say it?—a union, a camaraderie, a *fellowship* among us. Various ones would drift about the room, stretching their legs, and in whispered tones would ask, "How is your wife?" or "Do you have someone here too?"

In turn, they would share their stories, and there was an *immediate* empathy evidenced by facial expressions, extended arms, and concerned voices.

What created such a climate of openness and sharing among virtual strangers? It is like the church *should* be; yet it is a *struggle* in so many churches just to get a hello or a nod, let alone an expression of sincere concern!

I believe it was the *pain*—yes, the hurt, the concern, the sense of *shared* trauma and tragedy. Over and over I heard, "Yes, I know how you feel because my wife (or child or father) has that, too." A fellowship of concern. A fellowship of *shared hurt*.

I know, too, that this experience with Karen's cancer has brought the two of us closer together. After twenty-five years I've come to know you so well, I can almost always anticipate what you're thinking. I wouldn't have believed that I could love you more. Yet this has taught me new and beautiful things about you and to love you even more. What a miracle that out of pain comes beauty and love!

Prayer:

Teach me, O Lord, to share the burdens and hurts of others. Help us in our church relationships to be more caring . . . like You. Amen.

Now, Between the Two of You:

1. One of you read the selection above.
2. Share with each other ways in which you can share the hurts of others.

3. Read the Bible together. Use Hebrews 10:23-25.
4. In your prayer together, pray for the grace of encouragement to others.

Hebrews 10:23-25:

Let us hold unswervingly to the hope we profess, for he who promised is faithful. And let us consider how we may spur one another on toward love and good deeds. Let us not give up meeting together, as some are in the habit of doing, but let us encourage one another—and all the more as you see the Day approaching.

28. Transcending Barriers

I thought I'd write this letter while I'm "on the way" instead of headed back as usual. I hated to leave you all tonight. (I was tempted to call the group in Denver and delay the meeting!)

What a crowd! We hadn't had the kids all together like that since Steve went off to college four years ago; or, if so, I've forgotten it. Karen, Steve, and Philip, along with Ronny and little Wesley—all talking a mile a minute. Then that bunch of Philip's friends came in, and the stories began.

All of a sudden I looked up and there you were, sitting on the floor, right in the middle of them. They talked to you, laughed with you, and you with them! No generation gap visible! There were those in their teens and still in high school; Steve just out of college; Ronny in the business world; Karen, a young mother; Wesley, the grandchild—you and me.

You have that God-given ability to transcend every barrier, an ability I surely don't have. You are so approachable, so open, so spontaneous—with everybody! You have a unique way of relaxing everyone so that young people don't always think of you as an "adult."

With me, they don't forget that I'm older. And I

don't mind; that's just me. But I sure do enjoy watching you.

When I counted, there were fourteen people there. Their ages spanned from nineteen months to forty-four years and everyone of them knew they were "at home" *because of you.*

Thank you, dear one, you made my evening a delight. How I hated to leave. But I'll be back tomorrow night. Let's get together again!

Prayer:

> I Thank You, Lord, that barriers can be transcended and that oneness can be ours. Help me to be a bridge. Amen.

Now, Between the Two of You:

1. One of you read the selection above.
2. Share with each other:
   a. What barriers you need to transcend.
   b. How you can begin to overcome those barriers.
3. Read the Bible together. Use 2 Peter 1:5-8.
4. In your prayer together, thank the Lord for the challenge which barriers present and ask His help in transcending them.

2 Peter 1:5-8:

> *For this very reason, make every effort to add to your faith goodness; and to goodness, knowledge;*

and to knowledge, self-control; and to self-control, perseverance; and to perseverance, godliness; and to godliness, brotherly kindness; and to brotherly kindness, love. For if you possess these qualities in increasing measure, they will keep you from being ineffective and unproductive in your knowledge of our Lord Jesus Christ.

29. Hi, Dad!

Louisville is beautiful, and Philip is doing well at the basketball camp here. I got to see him play some in between the conferences I'm doing. He looks great!

There are about seventy-five other high school seniors who have been invited here with him for the week to be seen by college scouts. Philip is handling it well, too. He has real maturity about him. He will choose the right college, I'm sure.

It has been a long haul for Philip. He has wanted to be a basketball player since he was old enough to bounce a ball. I'm glad I was his first coach! Remember that YMCA league in Annapolis? I got to coach Steve for five years and then Philip for three. How I enjoyed that! (How I wish I had that energy now!)

In Philip I see a part of the boy I wished I could have been. He is the typical athlete (he'll probably wear his sneakers to his wedding!), yet is a National Honor Society student, senior class officer, and is active in the church youth group. That's a creditable combination!

I know that I would love him as much if he didn't play ball so well, but it is like icing on the cake that he does! How I enjoy watching him. I remember when I flew all night from Los Angeles just to see him play in that championship game.

Now his senior year is ahead of him, and with all the college scouts, he will have a heavier load to carry than ever.

I think we need to focus our prayers for him in a specific way. Let's pray that he will be at his best as he plays, that he will have special maturity as he deals with these scouts, and that his choice of a college will be a part of God's overall grand design for his life. I know that God has something more in mind for him, and his basketball and his college experience should fit into it.

Let's also pray that I'll do better with the referees this year!

P.S.—If he makes it to a college team and ever gets on TV, he'd better say, "Hi, *Dad*" (not "Mom" like most athletes do), too! After all, *I* am the one who taught him, took him to the games, and all!

Prayer:

> For the unique joys of parenthood, I thank You.
> For the unique responsibility of parenthood, I pray Your help. Amen.

Now, Between the Two of You:

1. One of you read the selection above.
2. Share with each other:
   a. The signs of maturity you see in your children.

   b. The plans you have to further enhance
      that maturity.
3. Read the Bible together. Use 2 Timothy
   2:1-9.
4. In your prayer, ask for divine wisdom in the
   role of developing maturity in others.

2 Timothy 2:1-9:

*You then, my son be strong in the grace that is in
Christ Jesus. And the things you have heard me say
in the presence of many witnesses entrust to reliable
men who will also be qualified to teach others. En-
dure hardship with us like a good soldier of Christ
Jesus. No one serving as a soldier gets involved in
civilian affairs—he wants to please his command-
ing officer. Similarly, if anyone competes as an
athlete, he does not receive the victor's crown unless
he competes according to the rules. The hard-
working farmer should be the first to receive a share
of the crops. Reflect on what I am saying, for the
Lord will give you insight into all this.*

*Remember Jesus Christ, raised from the dead,
descended from David. This is my gospel, for which
I am suffering even to the point of being chained like
a criminal. But God's word is not chained.*

30. Of Couples and Communion

It is late Sunday night here in Buenos Aires. One week of the trip is gone, and there is another yet to go. Tomorrow morning I leave for Rosario to train pastors and lay leaders in preparation for their crusade next fall. Over one thousand have already signed up for the conference!

As I've shared in my daily letters, this has been the most unforgettable week of my ministry so far. In contrast to most places I've been overseas, the spiritual hunger here is overwhelming. The seminary here holds this conference each year for the students during the day and at night includes the pastors. They have come from all over Argentina, some sleeping in tents in fifty-degree weather, and they literally pack the chapel at night.

The most unusual—and probably most unforgettable—event happened tonight. I spoke at the evening service of a church. It was a packed house—extra chairs were brought in and still some were left standing.

The pastor had planned a Communion service to follow my message. All went well until the cups were being distributed. I noticed a deacon come to the pastor at the altar and whisper to him. The pastor then spoke to us. All of the cups had been distributed and there were not enough to serve everyone! Then, with a stroke of wisdom and genius, he asked that the couples present share one cup between them so that the others might partake, too!

No only was it ingenious, it was beautiful. I thought, *This ought to be a planned event!*

I thought of you, too. How much I wanted you to be present! We've shared so many spiritual experiences together, but never this one. And we ought to!

Prayer:

> As we commune with You, O Lord, we also commune with each other. Help us to be ever closer to You and to each other. Amen.

Now, Between the Two of You:

1. One of you read the selection above.
2. Share with each other a memorable time of closeness together in worship.
3. Read the Bible together. Use Matthew 26:26-30.
4. In your prayer, thank God for the joys which come uniquely in worship together.

Matthew 26:26-30:

> *While they were eating, Jesus took bread, gave thanks and broke it, and gave it to his disciples, saying, "Take and eat; this is my body."*

Then he took the cup, gave thanks and offered it to them, saying "Drink from it, all of you. This is my blood of the covenant, which is poured out for many for the forgiveness of sins. I tell you, I will not drink of this fruit of the vine from now on until that day when I drink it anew with you in my Father's kingdom."

When they had sung a hymn, they went out to the Mount of Olives.

31. My Greatest Pride Is You

Hi! I'm putting this under your pillow. I know you'll be back shortly for a nap, and I thought I'd surprise you.

It's been like a dream come true here on this beautiful Caribbean island of Guadeloupe. I'm sitting on the veranda looking out over the ocean, and it is stupendous. Absolutely beautiful!

Only a moment ago, I looked up and saw you walking on the beach—and had to stop my reading and write you this quick note.

It's been a great twenty-five years, Aileen. We've looked forward to this trip to celebrate our "twenty-fifth" for so long, and now here we are. It has been a great trip and I hate to think about going home tomorrow. But, more than the great days we've had here, the twenty-five *years* we spent earning this time have been far, far greater.

I look back and marvel. It seems like only yesterday (I know that is a cliché, but it is true) that we were two kids in Dayton standing before dad at the altar for him to tie the knot. And he tied it tight enough to last a quarter of a century so far!

So many things have come and gone. Off to college. Karen born, then Steve, then Philip—each a "miracle." On to seminary and graduate school. Pastorates in Kentucky, Ohio, and Maryland. Schools and apartments and churches in six states in ten years! The early joys of parenthood—kindergarten plays, coaching the boys in basketball in YMCA leagues, seeing the kids become teenagers, Karen's wedding, college bills, trips together, and on and on.

Sadness, too, has come our way. Dad's death. Your father's recent passing. Karen's cancer. Your mother's illness. All a part of the fabric of our lives.

But as I look at you on the beach, my greatest pride, the greatest joy I feel, is you. How I love you!

You've come so far; you've given so much; you've accomplished so much and done it so well—your career, the children, the ministry of counseling, your spirit, your graciousness and kindly way of life, your wisdom—the list could go on almost endlessly.

Plus, you still look great!

So, I'll close. I'm going to wander off down the beach and find that perfect shell for you. I'll stick this under your pillow. Have a good nap. I love you!

Prayer:

Thank You, O Lord, that Your plans for my life included another's life and for the joy and help it has brought. Add more years to our joy and more joy to our years together. Amen.

Now, Between the Two of You:

1. One of you read the selection above.
2. Share with each other the joy and pride you

have in each other in specific ways and for specific reasons.

3. Read the Bible together. Use 1 Corinthians 13.

4. In your prayer, thank God for life and joy which are so much richer because of our mates.

1 Corinthians 13:

If I speak in the tongues of men and of angels, but have not love, I am only a resounding gong or a clanging cymbal. If I have the gift of prophecy and can fathom all mysteries and all knowledge, and if I have a faith that can move mountains, but have not love, I am nothing. If I give all I possess to the poor and surrender my body to the flames, but have not love, I gain nothing.

Love is patient, love is kind. It does not envy, it does not boast, it is not proud. It is not rude, it is not self-seeking, it is not easily angered, it keeps no record of wrongs. Love does not delight in evil but rejoices with the truth. It always protects, always trusts, always hopes, always perseveres.

Love never fails. But where there are prophecies, they will cease; where there are tongues, they will be stilled; where there is knowledge, it will pass away. For we know in part and we prophesy in part, but when perfection comes, the imperfect disappears. When I was a child, I talked like a child, I thought like a child, I reasoned like a child. When I became a man, I put childish ways behind me. Now we see but a poor reflection; then we shall see face to face. Now I know in part; then I shall know fully, even as I am fully known.

And now these three remain: faith, hope and love. But the greatest of these is love.

For contact regarding the ministry of the Haneys, corre-
spondence may be addressed to—

P.O. Box 28403
Memphis, TN 38128
(901) 372-2593